D0398530

The Hidden Gift of Christmas

...the cross of Christ

by Jane L. Fryar

The mission of CTA is
to glorify God by providing purposeful products
that lift up and encourage the body of Christ—
because we love him!

www.CTAinc.com

The Hidden Gift of Christmas

. . . the cross of Christ

by Jane L. Fryar

1625 Larkin Williams Rd.
Fenton, MO 63026

ISBN 978-1-935404-05-7

PRINTED IN THAILAND

The True Gift of Christmas

A hidden gift at Christmastime,
Concealed within the tree.
The cross of Christ where God's great love
Poured out for you and me!

TO:

____

FROM:

____

May God's great love fill your heart
with joy this Christmas!

The gift of God is eternal life
through Jesus Christ our Lord.

Romans 6:23 KJV

THE
HIDDEN GIFT
OF
CHRISTMAS

...the cross of Christ

AWAITING
THE GIFT . . .

Gifts!

Christmas gifts! Of every shape and size.
Wrapped in blue and gold and red.
All awaiting the happy hullabaloo, the jubilee
of Christmas Eve—and Christmas morning.

One Gift lies beneath the tree each year,
Toward the back—and all but forgotten.
Amidst the sparkling ornaments and bright packages.

A long-awaited Gift,
Most precious, yet often overlooked.
The greatest Gift of all.
The Hidden Gift of Christmas!

In the Beginning . . .

Christmas began in the heart of God before time.

Before starlight, before snowflakes,

before the first baby's smile.

Before it all . . .

Christmas warmed the heart of God.

God loved—always.

God loves—always.

And love gives.

Always!

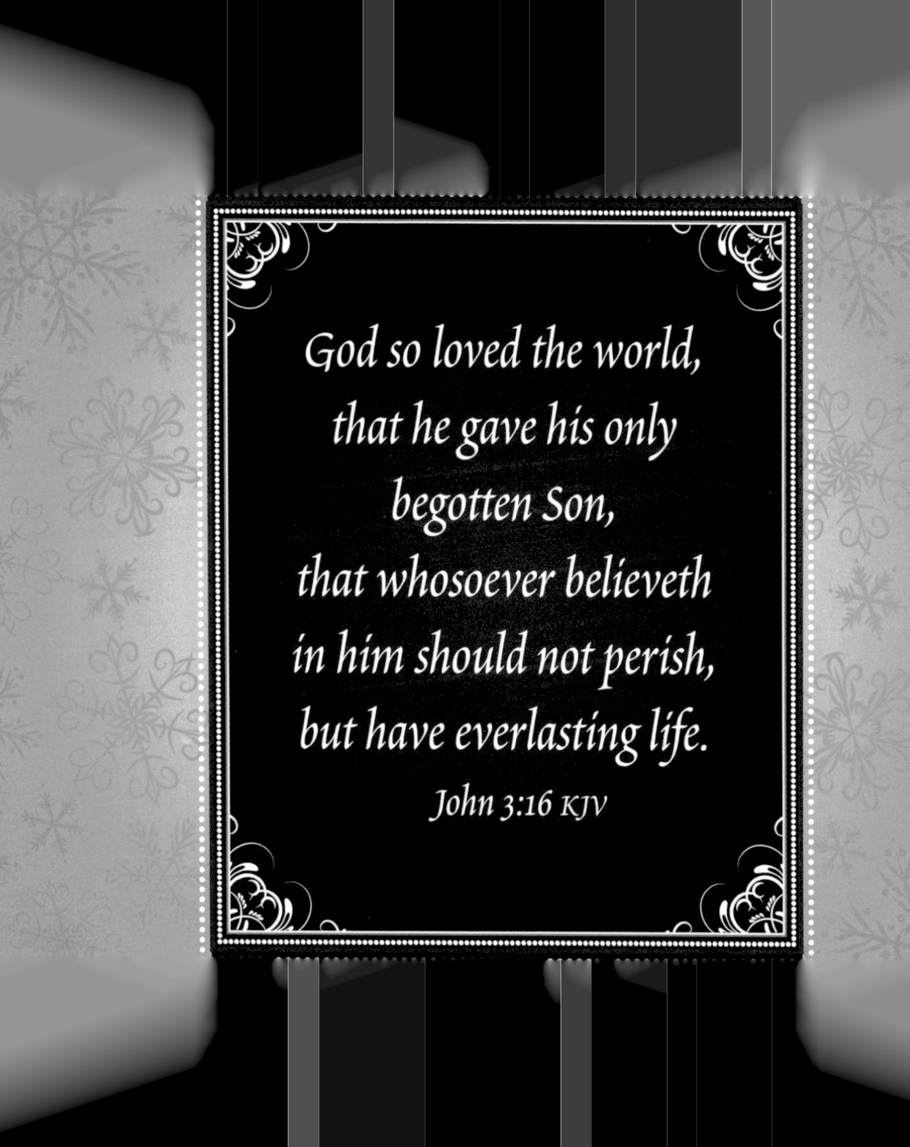
God so loved the world,
that he gave his only
begotten Son,
that whosoever believeth
in him should not perish,
but have everlasting life.
John 3:16 KJV

Waiting for Christmas

Waiting. Waiting. Waiting.
Waiting. Waiting. Waiting.

Remember how it felt when you were ten and
Christmas couldn't come soon enough?
That's how God's people long ago must have felt.
They waited.
Through decades . . .
Through centuries . . .
Through millenniums!

Waiting. Waiting. Waiting.

For Christmas. For the promised Savior.

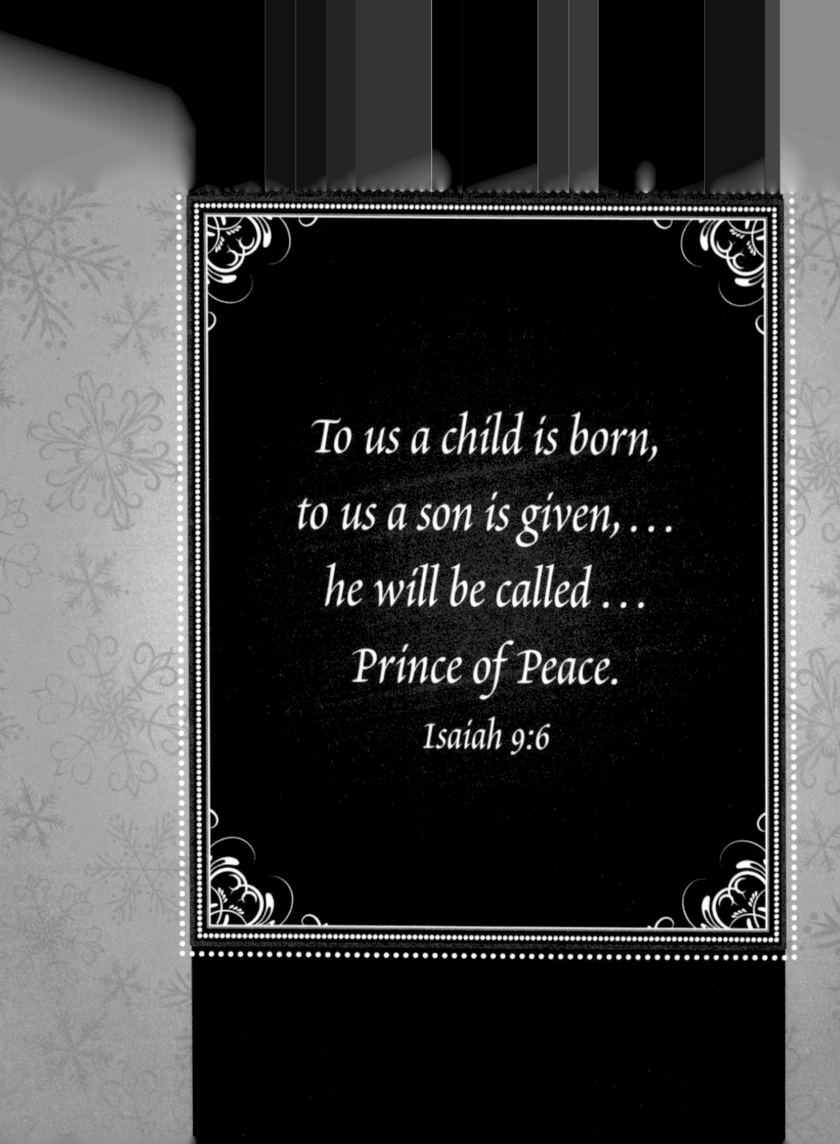
To us a child is born,
to us a son is given, . . .
he will be called . . .
Prince of Peace.
Isaiah 9:6

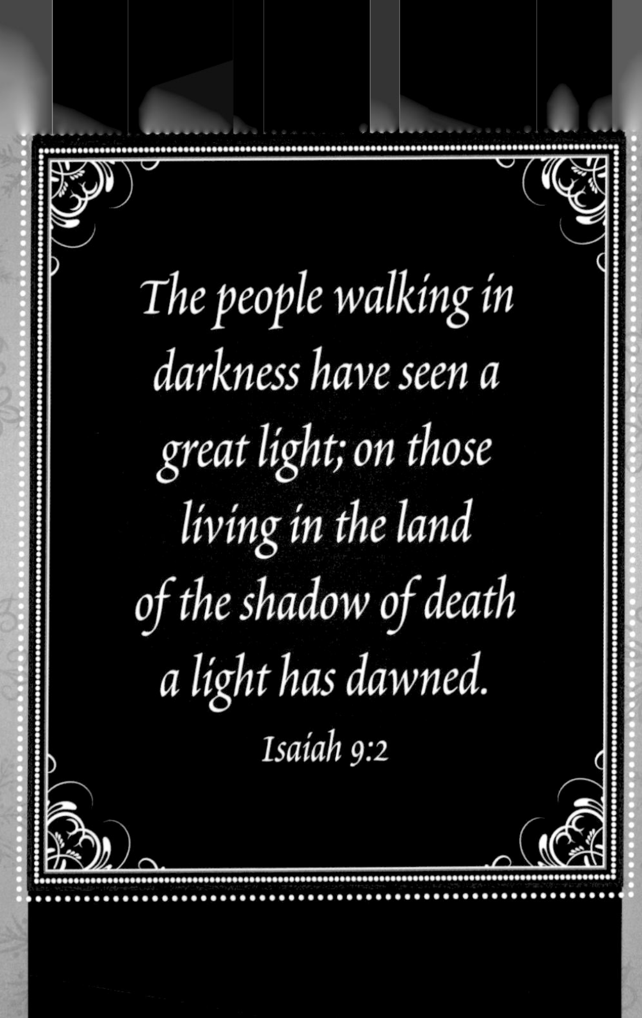
The people walking in
darkness have seen a
great light; on those
living in the land
of the shadow of death
a light has dawned.
Isaiah 9:2

The Lord himself will give you a sign: The virgin will be with child and will give birth to a son, and will call him Immanuel.

Isaiah 7:14

Surprise

There Gabriel stood—
in all his angelic glory,
Unexpected.
At Mary's elbow.

Surprise!

God's promise coming true,
The waiting finally over.

Surprise!

The virgin, about to bear a son.
Expecting, quite unexpectedly!

Surprise!

Immanuel—God with us!

The Holy Spirit will come
upon you, and the power
of the Most High will
overshadow you. So the
holy one to be born will
be called the Son of God.
Luke 1:35

Joseph

. . . knew every promise from of old,

. . . longed to see God's Word unfold,

. . . couldn't have guessed til he was told

. . . the part he'd play in grace so bold!

"Joseph son of David, do not be afraid to take Mary home as your wife, because what is conceived in her is from the Holy Spirit. She will give birth to a son, and you are to give him the name Jesus, because he will save his people from their sins."

Matthew 1:20–21

'Twas the Night before Christmas

Angels on tiptoes
Straining to see
God wrapping his Present
For you and for me!

When the time had fully come,
God sent his Son,
born of a woman,
born under law,
to redeem those under law,
that we might receive the
full rights of sons.

Galatians 4:4–5

THE HIDDEN GIFT OF CHRISTMAS

...the cross of Christ

UNWRAPPING
THE GIFT . . .

Gifts! Gifts!

Christmas gifts!
Delight wrapped up in a season
And decked out with a bow.

Christmas lights? Yes!
Christmas wreaths, garland, holly?
Yes. Yes. And yes!
Cookies and cocoa? Choirs and carols?
Yes, yes—a hundred times, yes!

But best of all, unwrapping the gifts.
Hearing tissue paper rip as ribbons fall away.

Best of all, unwrapping THE Gift,
The Gift God gave in love. So long ago:
The Hidden Gift of Christmas.

Once in Royal David's City

Once in royal David's city
Stood a lowly cattle shed,
Where a mother laid her baby
In a manger for his bed;
Mary was that mother mild,
Jesus Christ her little child.

He came down to earth from heaven
Who is God and Lord of all,
And his shelter was a stable,
And his cradle was a stall;
With the poor and mean and lowly,
Lived on earth our Savior holy.

Cecil F. Alexander, 1848

All this took place to fulfill what the Lord had said through the prophet: "The virgin will be with child and will give birth to a son, and they will call him Immanuel"—which means, "God with us."

Matthew 1:22–23

To Bethlehem, To See . . .

Angels filled the inky sky, then disappeared,
Leaving once-sleepy shepherds to rub their eyes
and cinch their robes more tightly about themselves
As they rushed off to see the sight the heavenly heralds
had trumpeted.

And what a sight! But not exactly what they'd had in mind.

No midwife. No cozy fire.
No fragrant, velvet blankets.
No royal palace guard.
God's Gift bundled up in strips of cloth,
red-faced and wailing on his mother's knee.

God with us—in diapers.

The shepherds had eyes
their King to see.

Do we?

When the angels had left them and gone into heaven, the shepherds said to one another, "Let's go to Bethlehem and see this thing that has happened, which the Lord has told us about."

Luke 2:15

Just Thinking (part one)

What did Mary think?
(What would you have thought?)

Smelly shepherds—back then, the lowest of the low.
Rumors of angels. And an angel choir!
Exhilaration invading the stable in the dead of night,
and dressed in burlap.

What did Mary think?!
(What would you have thought?)

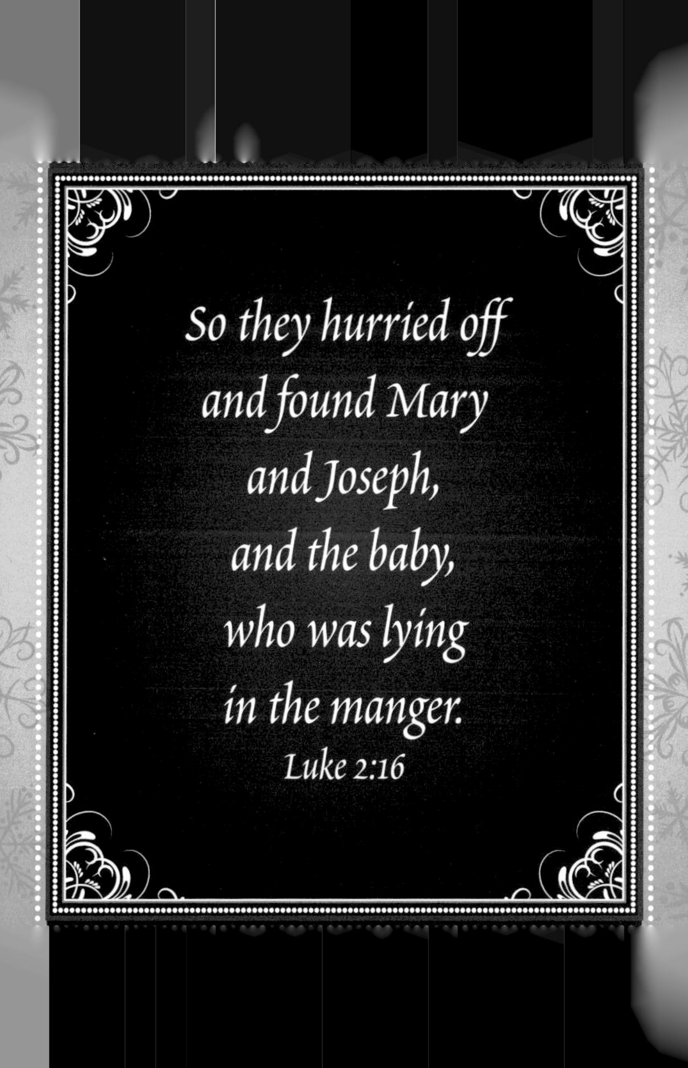
So they hurried off
and found Mary
and Joseph,
and the baby,
who was lying
in the manger.
Luke 2:16

Shepherds came to see
Then rushed away to tell,
Because the spell of God's eternal love
held their hearts enthralled.

Just so, seeing, we now kneel down to pray
Then rush away to share the bliss
to which we have been called.

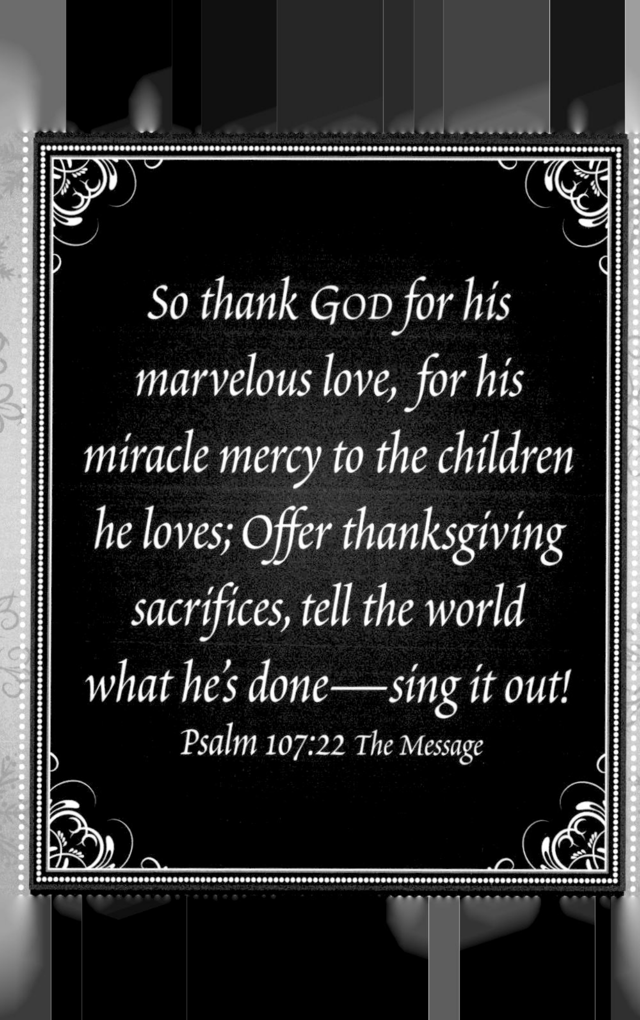
So thank GOD for his marvelous love, for his miracle mercy to the children he loves; Offer thanksgiving sacrifices, tell the world what he's done—sing it out!
Psalm 107:22 The Message

The Gift for Everyone

The Hidden Gift of Christmas
was just for Abraham
(but not just for Abraham).

It was just for ancient Israel
(but not just for ancient Israel).

It was just for first-century disciples
(but not just for them).

The Hidden Gift of Christmas, life now
and forever through Jesus the Savior,
was just for you,
just for me,
and fully, mercifully for everyone,
everywhere,
in every age!

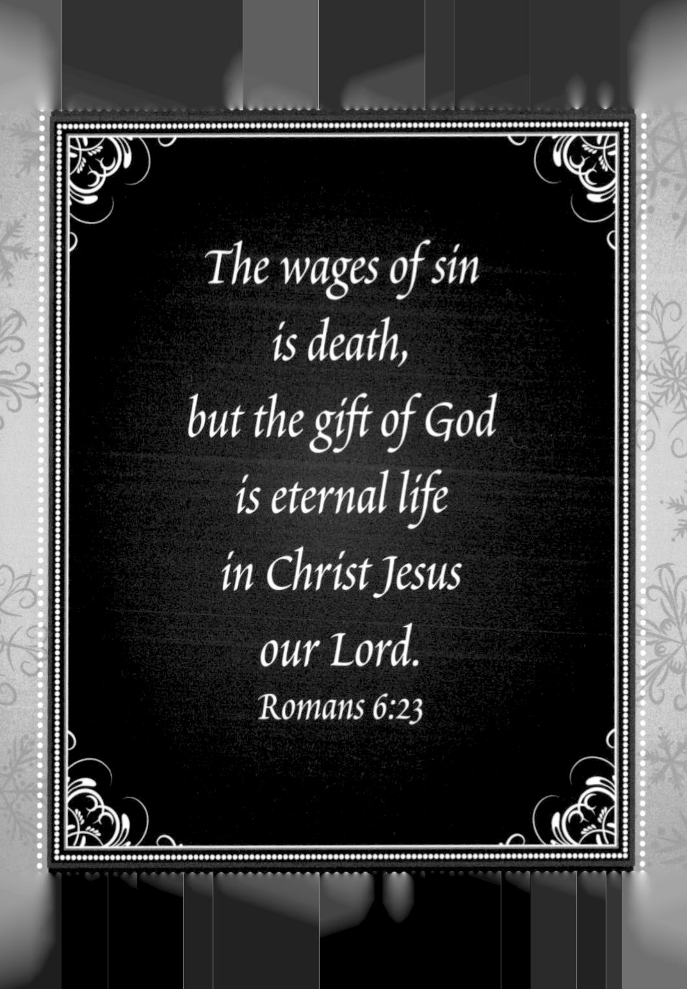
The wages of sin
is death,
but the gift of God
is eternal life
in Christ Jesus
our Lord.
Romans 6:23

Just Thinking (part two)

What did Mary think? (What would you have thought?)

Magi—majestic, mysterious,
 kneeling in wonder and in worship.

Gold! And frankincense, fit for a king!
Myrrh, fit for a Savior—fit for the Savior
 who would suffer and die.

What did Mary think?!
(What would you have thought?)

The star they had seen in the east went ahead of them until it stopped over the place where the child was. When they saw the star, they were overjoyed. On coming to the house, they saw the child with his mother Mary, and they bowed down and worshiped him. Then they opened their treasures and presented him with gifts of gold and of incense and of myrrh.

Matthew 2:9–11

THE HIDDEN GIFT OF CHRISTMAS

...the cross of Christ

SHARING
THE GIFT . . .

Christmas gifts! Delightfully unforgettable? Yes!
Unremarkably bland? Yes, that too, sometimes.

The engagement diamond from Christmas past
still changing the same two lives day by day.
The gray wool socks from Great Aunt Edna,
knitted with care and given with love,
this year, and every year yet again.

Gifts! Gifts! Gifts! But best of all, God's Gift.
The Gift once hidden, now revealed.
For all the world to see.

God's Gift! The Gift of Jesus.
The Gift of forgiveness and peace in his cross.
God's perfect Gift for Christmas giving!

Peace on Earth

Welcomed in snow-graced mountain chapels
and majestic, gargoyled cathedrals . . .
Remembered on far-flung battlefields and
in lonely prison cells . . .

Greeted by handbells,
children's carols, and
medieval chants,
or only the silence
of the stars . . .

Christmas comes,
and peace descends
in hearts
made new by the Christ Child.

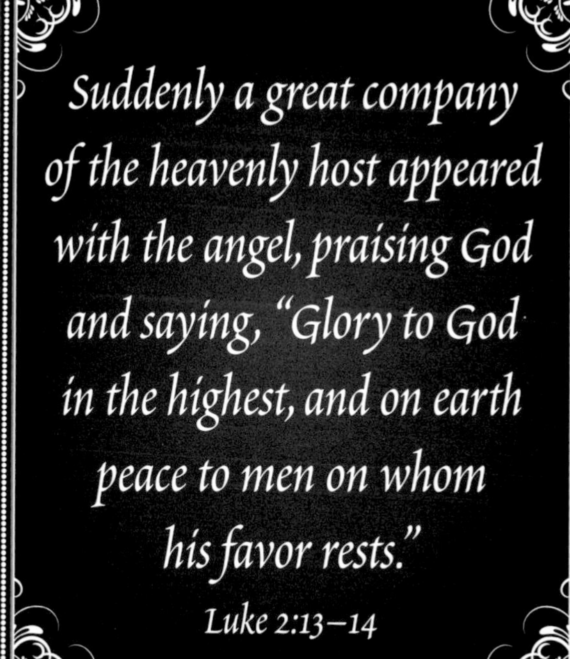
Suddenly a great company
of the heavenly host appeared
with the angel, praising God
and saying, "Glory to God
in the highest, and on earth
peace to men on whom
his favor rests."
Luke 2:13–14

It Came upon the Midnight Clear

It came upon the midnight clear,
That glorious song of old,
From angels bending near the earth
To touch their harps of gold:
"Peace on the earth, goodwill to men,
From heaven's all-gracious King!"
The world in solemn stillness lay
To hear the angels sing.

Still through the cloven skies they come
With peaceful wings unfurled,
And still their heavenly music floats
O'er all the weary world.
Above its sad and lowly plains
They bend on hovering wing,
And ever o'er its babel sounds
The blessed angels sing.

O you beneath life's crushing load,
Whose forms are bending low,
Who toil along the climbing way
With painful steps and slow;
Look now, for glad and golden hours
Come swiftly on the wing;
Oh rest beside the weary road
And hear the angels sing.

For lo, the days are hastening on,
By prophets seen of old,
When with the ever-circling years
Shall come the time foretold,
When the new heaven and earth shall own
The Prince of Peace, their King,
And the whole world send back the song
Which now the angels sing.

Edmund Hamilton Sears, 1849

Christmas Hope

Holding the Christ Child in our hearts

Opens the gateway to new dreams.

Possibilities, once unthinkable, brighten our thoughts.

Everything is changed by God's great Gift—the Gift of himself!

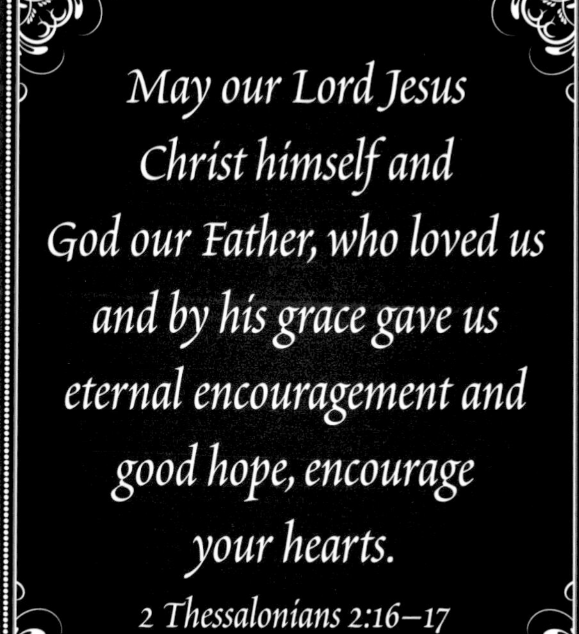
May our Lord Jesus
Christ himself and
God our Father, who loved us
and by his grace gave us
eternal encouragement and
good hope, encourage
your hearts.
2 Thessalonians 2:16–17

The Christmas Gift

The wrappings are off,
Fallen onto the floor.
The Gift, once a mystery,
Is hidden no more!

This Gift's meant for giving
And giving again.
So re-Gift and re-Gift
Til the world says, "Amen!"

This mystery
has been kept in the dark
for a long time, but now it's
out in the open....Christ is
in you, so therefore you can
look forward to sharing
in God's glory.
Colossians 1:26 The Message

A Joy for Sharing

An ordinary stable.
An ordinary stall.
But here God worked his miracles:
Christ born to save us all.

No earthquake, pomp, or splendor,
Just cattle standing near,
There God unleashed his mighty love—
We need no longer fear.

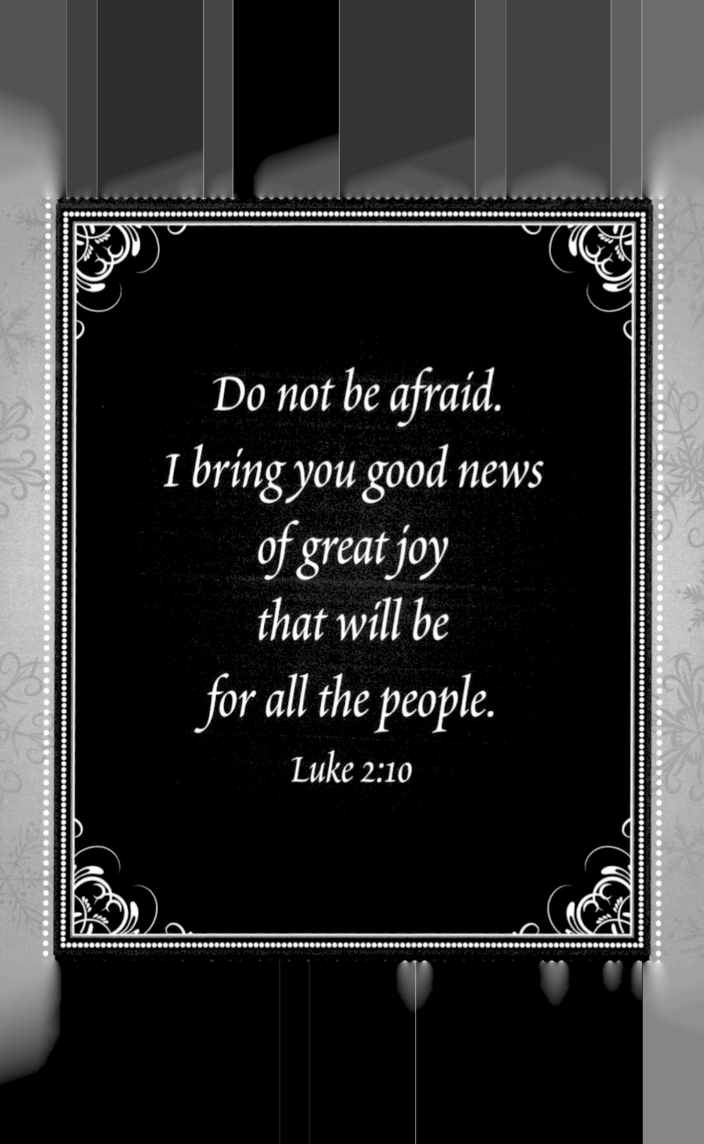
Do not be afraid.
I bring you good news
of great joy
that will be
for all the people.
Luke 2:10

Christ the Savior is born!

The Gift, once hidden, is now revealed.

Go, share this great news!

Merry Christmas!

Shout for joy to the LORD,
all the earth,
burst into jubilant song
with music;
make music to the
LORD with the harp,
with the harp and the
sound of singing.

Psalm 98:4–5

THE HIDDEN GIFT OF CHRISTMAS

...the cross of Christ

Silent Night, Holy Night

Silent night, holy night!
All is calm, all is bright
Round yon virgin mother and Child.
Holy Infant, so tender and mild,
Sleep in heavenly peace,
Sleep in heavenly peace.

Silent night, holy night!
Shepherds quake at the sight;
Glories stream from heaven afar,
Heavenly hosts sing, Alleluia!
Christ, the Savior, is born,
Christ, the Savior, is born!

Silent night, holy night,
Son of God, love's pure light
Radiant beams from thy holy face
With the dawn of redeeming grace,
Jesus, Lord, at thy birth,
Jesus, Lord, at thy birth.

Silent night, holy night
Wondrous star, lend thy light;
With the angels let us sing,
Alleluia to our King;
Christ, the Savior, is born,
Christ, the Savior, is born!

If this book has made a difference in your life or if you have simply enjoyed it, we would like to hear from you. Your words will encourage us! If you have suggestions for us to consider as we create books like this in the future, please send those, too.

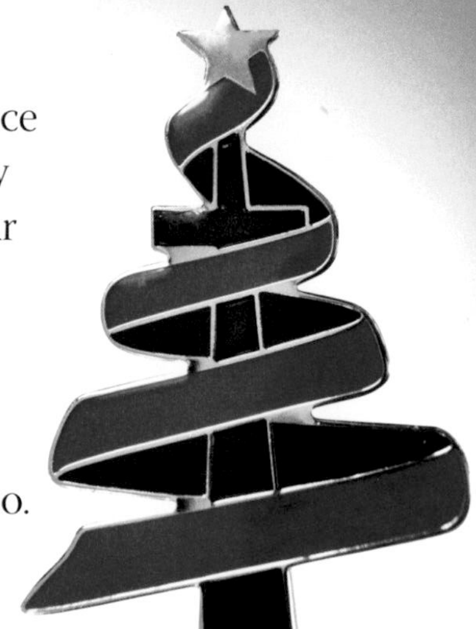

Send e-mail to editor@CTAinc.com and include the subject line: HGCXHC.

Write to Editorial Manager, Department HGCXHC, CTA, Inc. PO Box 1205, Fenton, MO 63026-1205.

Or leave a comment at share.CTAinc.com.